50 American Night Recipes for Home

By: Kelly Johnson

Table of Contents

- Spaghetti Aglio e Olio
- Bean and Cheese Quesadillas
- Veggie Stir-Fry with Rice
- One-Pot Pasta Primavera
- Lentil Soup
- Peanut Butter Banana Smoothie
- Homemade Macaroni and Cheese
- Chickpea Salad
- Tuna Pasta Salad
- Vegetable Curry with Rice
- Ramen Noodle Stir-Fry
- Black Bean Tacos
- Tomato and Basil Bruschetta
- Greek Yogurt Parfait with Granola and Fruit
- Baked Sweet Potato Fries
- Quinoa Salad with Veggies
- Hummus and Veggie Wraps
- Baked Ziti with Vegetables
- Egg Fried Rice
- Avocado Toast with Egg
- Broccoli and Cheese Stuffed Baked Potatoes
- Homemade Pizza with Tortilla Crust
- Caprese Salad
- Grilled Cheese Sandwiches
- Veggie Omelette
- Pasta with Marinara Sauce
- Oatmeal with Fruit and Nuts
- Tofu Stir-Fry with Noodles
- Black Bean Soup
- Couscous Salad with Chickpeas and Veggies
- Mexican Rice and Beans
- Spinach and Feta Quesadillas
- Baked Chicken Drumsticks
- Pancakes with Maple Syrup
- Tomato and Mozzarella Panini

- Pita Bread Pizzas
- Creamy Mushroom Risotto
- Banana Bread
- Corn and Black Bean Salad
- Vegetable Frittata
- Potato and Pea Curry
- Egg Salad Sandwiches
- Stuffed Bell Peppers
- Tuna Melt Sandwiches
- Three Bean Chili
- Mashed Potatoes with Gravy
- Tofu Scramble with Spinach
- Peanut Noodles
- Rice and Beans Burritos
- Baked Falafel Wraps

Spaghetti Aglio e Olio

Ingredients:

- 8 ounces spaghetti
- 4 cloves garlic, thinly sliced
- 1/4 cup extra virgin olive oil
- 1/2 teaspoon red pepper flakes (adjust to taste)
- Salt, to taste
- Freshly ground black pepper, to taste
- Fresh parsley, chopped, for garnish
- Grated Parmesan cheese, for serving (optional)

Instructions:

1. Cook the spaghetti in a large pot of salted boiling water until al dente, according to the package instructions. Reserve about 1/2 cup of pasta cooking water, then drain the spaghetti.
2. While the spaghetti is cooking, heat the olive oil in a large skillet over medium heat. Add the sliced garlic and red pepper flakes. Cook, stirring frequently, until the garlic is golden brown and fragrant, about 1-2 minutes. Be careful not to burn the garlic.
3. Add the cooked spaghetti to the skillet with the garlic and oil. Toss to coat the spaghetti evenly with the garlic-infused oil. If the pasta seems dry, add some of the reserved pasta cooking water to loosen it up.
4. Season the spaghetti with salt and freshly ground black pepper, to taste. Toss once more to combine.
5. Remove the skillet from the heat and transfer the spaghetti to serving plates. Garnish with chopped fresh parsley and grated Parmesan cheese, if desired.
6. Serve immediately, while hot. Enjoy your Spaghetti Aglio e Olio!

This dish is quick, easy, and packed with flavor, making it perfect for busy college students on a budget.

Bean and Cheese Quesadillas

Ingredients:

- 4 large flour tortillas
- 1 can (15 ounces) of black beans, drained and rinsed
- 1 cup shredded cheese (such as cheddar, Monterey Jack, or a Mexican blend)
- 1/2 cup diced tomatoes (optional)
- 1/4 cup diced onions (optional)
- 1/4 cup chopped cilantro (optional)
- Salt and pepper, to taste
- Cooking spray or oil, for cooking

Instructions:

1. Heat a large skillet over medium heat.
2. Place one tortilla in the skillet. Spread a quarter of the black beans evenly over half of the tortilla.
3. Sprinkle a quarter of the shredded cheese over the beans.
4. If using, sprinkle diced tomatoes, onions, and cilantro over the cheese.
5. Season with salt and pepper, to taste.
6. Fold the tortilla in half over the filling, creating a half-moon shape.
7. Press down gently with a spatula to help the quesadilla hold together.
8. Cook for 2-3 minutes on each side, or until the tortilla is golden brown and crispy, and the cheese is melted.
9. Remove the quesadilla from the skillet and place it on a cutting board. Allow it to cool for a minute before cutting into wedges.
10. Repeat with the remaining tortillas and filling ingredients.
11. Serve the bean and cheese quesadillas warm, with salsa, guacamole, sour cream, or your favorite dipping sauce on the side.

Enjoy your homemade bean and cheese quesadillas! They're customizable, satisfying, and budget-friendly.

Veggie Stir-Fry with Rice

Ingredients:

- 1 cup uncooked rice (white or brown)
- 2 tablespoons vegetable oil
- 2 cloves garlic, minced
- 1 small onion, thinly sliced
- 2 cups mixed vegetables (such as bell peppers, broccoli, carrots, snap peas, mushrooms, etc.), chopped
- 1/4 cup soy sauce (or tamari for gluten-free option)
- 2 tablespoons rice vinegar
- 1 tablespoon honey or maple syrup
- 1 teaspoon sesame oil (optional)
- 1 tablespoon cornstarch (or arrowroot powder) mixed with 2 tablespoons water (to thicken sauce)
- Sesame seeds and sliced green onions, for garnish (optional)

Instructions:

1. Cook the rice according to package instructions. Once cooked, set aside and keep warm.
2. In a large skillet or wok, heat the vegetable oil over medium-high heat.
3. Add the minced garlic and sliced onion to the skillet. Stir-fry for 1-2 minutes, or until the onion is translucent and fragrant.
4. Add the mixed vegetables to the skillet. Stir-fry for 3-4 minutes, or until the vegetables are tender-crisp.
5. In a small bowl, whisk together the soy sauce, rice vinegar, honey or maple syrup, and sesame oil (if using).
6. Pour the sauce over the vegetables in the skillet. Stir to coat the vegetables evenly with the sauce.
7. In a separate small bowl, mix together the cornstarch (or arrowroot powder) and water to create a slurry.
8. Add the cornstarch slurry to the skillet, stirring constantly. Cook for an additional 1-2 minutes, or until the sauce has thickened.
9. Remove the skillet from the heat.
10. Serve the veggie stir-fry over the cooked rice.
11. Garnish with sesame seeds and sliced green onions, if desired.

12. Enjoy your delicious and nutritious veggie stir-fry with rice!

Feel free to customize this recipe by adding tofu, tempeh, or your favorite protein for an extra boost of flavor and nutrition.

One-Pot Pasta Primavera

Ingredients:

- 8 ounces pasta (such as penne or fettuccine)
- 2 cups mixed vegetables (such as bell peppers, cherry tomatoes, zucchini, broccoli, carrots, etc.), chopped
- 2 cloves garlic, minced
- 4 cups vegetable broth (or chicken broth if not vegetarian)
- 1 cup heavy cream (or coconut milk for a dairy-free option)
- 1/2 cup grated Parmesan cheese (optional)
- 2 tablespoons olive oil
- 1 tablespoon Italian seasoning (or a mixture of dried basil, oregano, and thyme)
- Salt and pepper, to taste
- Fresh parsley, chopped, for garnish (optional)

Instructions:

1. In a large pot or Dutch oven, heat the olive oil over medium heat.
2. Add the minced garlic to the pot and cook for 1-2 minutes, or until fragrant.
3. Add the pasta and mixed vegetables to the pot.
4. Pour the vegetable broth over the pasta and vegetables. Bring to a boil.
5. Reduce the heat to low and simmer, stirring occasionally, until the pasta is cooked and the vegetables are tender, about 10-12 minutes.
6. Stir in the heavy cream (or coconut milk) and Italian seasoning. Cook for an additional 2-3 minutes, or until heated through.
7. If using, stir in the grated Parmesan cheese until melted and creamy.
8. Season with salt and pepper, to taste.
9. Remove the pot from the heat.
10. Serve the one-pot pasta primavera hot, garnished with fresh parsley, if desired.

Enjoy your delicious and colorful one-pot pasta primavera! It's a satisfying meal that's perfect for busy weeknights.

Lentil Soup

Ingredients:

- 1 cup dried lentils (brown or green), rinsed and picked over
- 1 onion, diced
- 2 carrots, diced
- 2 celery stalks, diced
- 3 cloves garlic, minced
- 6 cups vegetable broth (or chicken broth if not vegetarian)
- 1 can (14.5 ounces) diced tomatoes
- 1 teaspoon ground cumin
- 1 teaspoon ground coriander
- 1/2 teaspoon smoked paprika
- Salt and pepper, to taste
- 2 tablespoons olive oil
- Fresh parsley or cilantro, chopped, for garnish (optional)
- Lemon wedges, for serving (optional)

Instructions:

1. In a large pot or Dutch oven, heat the olive oil over medium heat.
2. Add the diced onion, carrots, and celery to the pot. Cook, stirring occasionally, until the vegetables are softened, about 5 minutes.
3. Add the minced garlic to the pot and cook for an additional 1-2 minutes, or until fragrant.
4. Stir in the dried lentils, vegetable broth, diced tomatoes (with their juices), ground cumin, ground coriander, and smoked paprika.
5. Bring the soup to a boil, then reduce the heat to low. Cover and simmer for 20-25 minutes, or until the lentils are tender.
6. Season the soup with salt and pepper, to taste.
7. If desired, use an immersion blender to partially blend the soup for a thicker consistency. Alternatively, transfer a portion of the soup to a blender and blend until smooth, then return it to the pot.
8. Taste and adjust the seasoning if needed.
9. Ladle the lentil soup into bowls and garnish with chopped fresh parsley or cilantro, if desired.
10. Serve hot, with lemon wedges on the side for squeezing over the soup.

Enjoy your hearty and flavorful lentil soup! It's perfect for a cozy meal any time of the year.

Peanut Butter Banana Smoothie

Ingredients:

- 1 ripe banana, peeled and sliced
- 2 tablespoons peanut butter (creamy or crunchy)
- 1/2 cup plain Greek yogurt (or dairy-free yogurt for a vegan option)
- 1/2 cup milk (dairy or plant-based)
- 1 tablespoon honey or maple syrup (optional, for added sweetness)
- 1/2 teaspoon vanilla extract (optional)
- 1/2 cup ice cubes

Instructions:

1. Place all the ingredients in a blender.
2. Blend on high speed until smooth and creamy, scraping down the sides of the blender as needed.
3. Taste the smoothie and adjust the sweetness or thickness by adding more honey or milk if desired.
4. Once the smoothie reaches your desired consistency, pour it into glasses.
5. Serve immediately and enjoy your peanut butter banana smoothie!

You can also customize this recipe by adding a handful of spinach or kale for extra nutrients, a scoop of protein powder for an added protein boost, or a sprinkle of cinnamon for extra flavor. Feel free to get creative and make it your own!

Homemade Macaroni and Cheese

Ingredients:

- 8 ounces elbow macaroni or pasta of your choice
- 2 tablespoons butter
- 2 tablespoons all-purpose flour
- 2 cups milk
- 2 cups shredded cheese (such as cheddar, Gruyere, or a blend)
- 1/2 teaspoon salt
- 1/4 teaspoon black pepper
- 1/4 teaspoon paprika (optional)
- 1/4 cup breadcrumbs (optional, for topping)

Instructions:

1. Preheat your oven to 350°F (175°C). Grease a baking dish or casserole dish and set aside.
2. Cook the macaroni according to the package instructions until al dente. Drain and set aside.
3. In a large saucepan, melt the butter over medium heat.
4. Stir in the flour and cook for 1-2 minutes, stirring constantly, until the mixture is smooth and bubbly.
5. Gradually whisk in the milk, stirring constantly to prevent lumps from forming.
6. Cook the sauce, stirring frequently, until it thickens, about 5-7 minutes.
7. Stir in the shredded cheese until melted and smooth. Season with salt, pepper, and paprika, if using.
8. Add the cooked macaroni to the cheese sauce and stir until well combined.
9. Pour the macaroni and cheese mixture into the prepared baking dish, spreading it out evenly.
10. If desired, sprinkle breadcrumbs evenly over the top of the macaroni and cheese.
11. Bake in the preheated oven for 25-30 minutes, or until the top is golden brown and the cheese is bubbly.
12. Remove from the oven and let it cool for a few minutes before serving.
13. Serve your homemade macaroni and cheese hot, garnished with additional cheese or herbs if desired.

Enjoy your creamy and delicious homemade macaroni and cheese! It's a comforting dish that's perfect for any occasion.

Chickpea Salad

Ingredients:

- 2 cans (15 ounces each) chickpeas (garbanzo beans), drained and rinsed
- 1 cucumber, diced
- 1 bell pepper (any color), diced
- 1/2 red onion, finely chopped
- 1/4 cup chopped fresh parsley
- 1/4 cup chopped fresh cilantro (optional)
- 2 tablespoons extra virgin olive oil
- 2 tablespoons lemon juice (or vinegar of your choice)
- 1 teaspoon ground cumin
- Salt and pepper, to taste

Instructions:

1. In a large mixing bowl, combine the drained and rinsed chickpeas, diced cucumber, diced bell pepper, finely chopped red onion, chopped fresh parsley, and chopped fresh cilantro (if using).
2. In a small bowl, whisk together the extra virgin olive oil, lemon juice (or vinegar), ground cumin, salt, and pepper to make the dressing.
3. Pour the dressing over the chickpea salad ingredients in the large mixing bowl.
4. Toss gently to coat all the ingredients evenly with the dressing.
5. Taste and adjust the seasoning, adding more salt, pepper, or lemon juice as needed.
6. Cover the bowl and refrigerate the chickpea salad for at least 30 minutes to allow the flavors to meld.
7. Before serving, give the salad a final toss and adjust the seasoning if needed.
8. Serve the chickpea salad chilled, as a side dish or a light main course.

Enjoy your refreshing and flavorful chickpea salad! It's perfect for picnics, potlucks, or as a healthy lunch option.

Tuna Pasta Salad

Ingredients:

- 8 ounces pasta (such as rotini, penne, or fusilli)
- 2 cans (5 ounces each) tuna, drained
- 1/2 cup mayonnaise
- 1/4 cup plain Greek yogurt (or sour cream)
- 2 tablespoons lemon juice
- 1 teaspoon Dijon mustard
- 1/2 cup diced celery
- 1/2 cup diced red bell pepper
- 1/4 cup diced red onion
- 1/4 cup chopped fresh parsley
- Salt and pepper, to taste
- Optional add-ins: diced cucumber, shredded carrots, chopped olives, diced tomatoes, etc.

Instructions:

1. Cook the pasta according to the package instructions until al dente. Drain and rinse under cold water to cool. Transfer to a large mixing bowl.
2. Add the drained tuna to the bowl with the cooked pasta.
3. In a small bowl, whisk together the mayonnaise, Greek yogurt, lemon juice, and Dijon mustard until smooth.
4. Pour the dressing over the pasta and tuna in the mixing bowl.
5. Add the diced celery, diced red bell pepper, diced red onion, and chopped fresh parsley to the bowl.
6. Toss gently to coat all the ingredients evenly with the dressing.
7. Taste and adjust the seasoning, adding salt and pepper as needed.
8. If desired, add any optional add-ins to the salad and toss again to combine.
9. Cover the bowl and refrigerate the tuna pasta salad for at least 30 minutes to allow the flavors to meld.
10. Before serving, give the salad a final toss and adjust the seasoning if needed.
11. Serve the tuna pasta salad chilled, garnished with additional chopped parsley or lemon wedges if desired.

Enjoy your delicious and customizable tuna pasta salad! It's perfect for picnics, potlucks, or meal prep lunches.

Vegetable Curry with Rice

Ingredients:

For the curry:

- 2 tablespoons vegetable oil
- 1 onion, diced
- 2 cloves garlic, minced
- 1 tablespoon grated ginger
- 2 tablespoons curry powder
- 1 teaspoon ground turmeric
- 1 teaspoon ground cumin
- 1 teaspoon ground coriander
- 1/2 teaspoon chili powder (adjust to taste)
- 1 can (14 ounces) coconut milk
- 1 cup vegetable broth
- 2 cups mixed vegetables (such as bell peppers, carrots, potatoes, peas, cauliflower, etc.), chopped
- Salt and pepper, to taste
- Fresh cilantro, chopped, for garnish (optional)

For the rice:

- 1 cup long-grain white rice (such as jasmine or basmati)
- 2 cups water
- 1/2 teaspoon salt

Instructions:

1. In a large skillet or saucepan, heat the vegetable oil over medium heat.
2. Add the diced onion to the skillet and cook until softened and translucent, about 5 minutes.
3. Stir in the minced garlic and grated ginger, and cook for an additional 1-2 minutes, until fragrant.
4. Add the curry powder, ground turmeric, ground cumin, ground coriander, and chili powder to the skillet. Stir to toast the spices for about 1 minute.
5. Pour in the coconut milk and vegetable broth, stirring to combine.
6. Add the chopped mixed vegetables to the skillet. Bring the mixture to a simmer.

7. Reduce the heat to low, cover the skillet, and let the curry simmer for about 15-20 minutes, or until the vegetables are tender.
8. While the curry is simmering, prepare the rice. Rinse the rice under cold water until the water runs clear, then drain.
9. In a separate pot, bring 2 cups of water to a boil. Stir in the rinsed rice and salt.
10. Reduce the heat to low, cover the pot, and let the rice simmer for about 15-20 minutes, or until the water is absorbed and the rice is tender.
11. Once the curry and rice are cooked, season the curry with salt and pepper to taste.
12. Serve the vegetable curry over the cooked rice.
13. Garnish with fresh chopped cilantro, if desired.
14. Enjoy your delicious vegetable curry with rice!

This dish is versatile, so feel free to customize it by adding your favorite vegetables or adjusting the spices to your taste preferences.

Ramen Noodle Stir-Fry

Ingredients:

- 2 packs of ramen noodles (discard the seasoning packets)
- 2 tablespoons vegetable oil
- 2 cloves garlic, minced
- 1 small onion, thinly sliced
- 2 cups mixed vegetables (such as bell peppers, broccoli, carrots, snap peas, mushrooms, etc.), chopped
- 1/4 cup soy sauce
- 2 tablespoons hoisin sauce
- 1 tablespoon rice vinegar
- 1 teaspoon sesame oil
- 1 teaspoon grated ginger (optional)
- 1/4 teaspoon red pepper flakes (optional)
- Green onions, chopped, for garnish
- Sesame seeds, for garnish

Instructions:

1. Cook the ramen noodles according to the package instructions. Drain and set aside.
2. In a large skillet or wok, heat the vegetable oil over medium-high heat.
3. Add the minced garlic and thinly sliced onion to the skillet. Cook for 1-2 minutes, or until the onion is softened and fragrant.
4. Add the mixed vegetables to the skillet. Stir-fry for 3-4 minutes, or until the vegetables are tender-crisp.
5. In a small bowl, whisk together the soy sauce, hoisin sauce, rice vinegar, sesame oil, grated ginger (if using), and red pepper flakes (if using).
6. Add the cooked ramen noodles to the skillet.
7. Pour the sauce over the noodles and vegetables in the skillet.
8. Toss everything together until well combined and heated through.
9. Remove the skillet from the heat.
10. Serve the ramen noodle stir-fry hot, garnished with chopped green onions and sesame seeds.

Enjoy your delicious and flavorful ramen noodle stir-fry! It's a quick and easy meal that's sure to satisfy.

Black Bean Tacos

Ingredients:

- 1 can (15 ounces) black beans, drained and rinsed
- 1 tablespoon olive oil
- 1/2 onion, diced
- 2 cloves garlic, minced
- 1 teaspoon ground cumin
- 1 teaspoon chili powder
- Salt and pepper, to taste
- 8 small corn or flour tortillas
- Toppings of your choice: shredded lettuce, diced tomatoes, sliced avocado, salsa, cilantro, lime wedges, etc.

Instructions:

1. Heat the olive oil in a large skillet over medium heat.
2. Add the diced onion to the skillet and cook until softened, about 3-4 minutes.
3. Add the minced garlic to the skillet and cook for an additional minute, until fragrant.
4. Stir in the drained and rinsed black beans, ground cumin, chili powder, salt, and pepper.
5. Cook, stirring occasionally, for 5-7 minutes, or until the beans are heated through and the flavors have melded.
6. While the beans are cooking, warm the tortillas according to the package instructions.
7. Once the beans are ready, assemble the tacos by spooning the black bean mixture onto each tortilla.
8. Top the tacos with your favorite toppings, such as shredded lettuce, diced tomatoes, sliced avocado, salsa, cilantro, and a squeeze of lime juice.
9. Serve the black bean tacos immediately, with extra toppings on the side if desired.

Enjoy your flavorful and nutritious black bean tacos! They're perfect for a quick and easy weeknight dinner or for a fun taco night with friends and family.

Tomato and Basil Bruschetta

Ingredients:

- 4-6 ripe tomatoes, diced
- 1/4 cup fresh basil leaves, thinly sliced
- 2 cloves garlic, minced
- 2 tablespoons extra virgin olive oil
- 1 tablespoon balsamic vinegar (optional)
- Salt and pepper, to taste
- 1 baguette or Italian bread, sliced
- Olive oil, for brushing
- Optional toppings: grated Parmesan cheese, balsamic glaze, chopped olives, etc.

Instructions:

1. In a medium mixing bowl, combine the diced tomatoes, thinly sliced basil leaves, minced garlic, extra virgin olive oil, and balsamic vinegar (if using).
2. Season the tomato mixture with salt and pepper to taste. Stir to combine all the ingredients evenly.
3. Let the tomato mixture marinate for at least 15-20 minutes to allow the flavors to meld.
4. While the tomato mixture is marinating, preheat your oven broiler or grill.
5. Brush the sliced baguette or Italian bread with olive oil on both sides.
6. Place the bread slices under the broiler or on the grill and cook for 1-2 minutes on each side, until lightly toasted and golden brown.
7. Remove the toasted bread from the oven or grill and let it cool slightly.
8. Once cooled, spoon the tomato and basil mixture generously onto each toasted bread slice.
9. If desired, sprinkle grated Parmesan cheese over the top of each bruschetta.
10. Drizzle with balsamic glaze or top with chopped olives for extra flavor, if desired.
11. Serve the tomato and basil bruschetta immediately as a delicious appetizer or snack.

Enjoy your flavorful and aromatic tomato and basil bruschetta! It's a perfect appetizer for summer gatherings or anytime you're craving a taste of Italy.

Greek Yogurt Parfait with Granola and Fruit

Ingredients:

- 1 cup Greek yogurt (plain or flavored)
- 1/2 cup granola (store-bought or homemade)
- 1/2 cup fresh fruit (such as berries, sliced bananas, diced peaches, etc.)
- Honey or maple syrup, for drizzling (optional)

Instructions:

1. In a serving glass or bowl, spoon a layer of Greek yogurt into the bottom.
2. Add a layer of granola on top of the yogurt.
3. Top the granola with a layer of fresh fruit.
4. Repeat the layers until you've used up all the ingredients or reached the desired amount.
5. If desired, drizzle honey or maple syrup over the top for added sweetness.
6. Serve the Greek yogurt parfait immediately and enjoy!

You can customize this recipe by using your favorite flavor of Greek yogurt, choosing your preferred type of granola (such as oats, nuts, seeds, etc.), and selecting your favorite fruits. It's a versatile and satisfying dish that's perfect for breakfast or a healthy snack on the go.

Baked Sweet Potato Fries

Ingredients:

- 2 medium sweet potatoes, scrubbed and dried
- 2 tablespoons olive oil
- 1 teaspoon paprika
- 1/2 teaspoon garlic powder
- 1/2 teaspoon onion powder
- 1/4 teaspoon cayenne pepper (optional, for a spicy kick)
- Salt and pepper, to taste
- Optional dipping sauce: ketchup, aioli, sriracha mayo, etc.

Instructions:

1. Preheat your oven to 425°F (220°C) and line a baking sheet with parchment paper or aluminum foil for easy cleanup.
2. Cut the sweet potatoes into thin strips or wedges, about 1/4 to 1/2 inch thick.
3. In a large bowl, toss the sweet potato strips with olive oil until evenly coated.
4. In a small bowl, mix together the paprika, garlic powder, onion powder, cayenne pepper (if using), salt, and pepper.
5. Sprinkle the spice mixture over the sweet potatoes and toss until the fries are evenly coated with the seasonings.
6. Arrange the sweet potato fries in a single layer on the prepared baking sheet, making sure they're not overlapping.
7. Bake in the preheated oven for 20-25 minutes, flipping halfway through, or until the fries are golden brown and crispy.
8. Once done, remove the baking sheet from the oven and let the sweet potato fries cool slightly before serving.
9. Serve the baked sweet potato fries hot, with your favorite dipping sauce on the side.

Enjoy your delicious and healthier baked sweet potato fries as a side dish or snack! They're crispy on the outside, tender on the inside, and bursting with flavor.

Quinoa Salad with Veggies

Ingredients:

- 1 cup quinoa, rinsed
- 2 cups water or vegetable broth
- 1 cup cherry tomatoes, halved
- 1 cucumber, diced
- 1 bell pepper (any color), diced
- 1/4 cup red onion, finely chopped
- 1/4 cup fresh parsley, chopped
- 1/4 cup fresh mint leaves, chopped (optional)
- 1/4 cup crumbled feta cheese (optional)
- Juice of 1 lemon
- 2 tablespoons extra virgin olive oil
- Salt and pepper, to taste

Instructions:

1. In a medium saucepan, combine the quinoa and water or vegetable broth. Bring to a boil over medium-high heat.
2. Reduce the heat to low, cover, and simmer for 15-20 minutes, or until the quinoa is cooked and the liquid is absorbed. Remove from heat and let it cool.
3. In a large mixing bowl, combine the cooked quinoa, halved cherry tomatoes, diced cucumber, diced bell pepper, finely chopped red onion, chopped parsley, and chopped mint leaves (if using).
4. In a small bowl, whisk together the lemon juice and extra virgin olive oil to make the dressing.
5. Pour the dressing over the quinoa and vegetable mixture in the mixing bowl. Toss gently to combine.
6. If using, sprinkle crumbled feta cheese over the salad and toss again.
7. Season the quinoa salad with salt and pepper to taste.
8. Cover the bowl and refrigerate the quinoa salad for at least 30 minutes to allow the flavors to meld.
9. Before serving, give the salad a final toss and adjust the seasoning if needed.
10. Serve the quinoa salad with veggies chilled or at room temperature.

Enjoy your delicious and nutritious quinoa salad with veggies! It's packed with protein, fiber, and vitamins, making it a perfect option for a healthy meal.

Hummus and Veggie Wraps

Ingredients:

- 4 large whole wheat or spinach wraps/tortillas
- 1 cup hummus (store-bought or homemade)
- 2 cups mixed vegetables (such as shredded carrots, sliced cucumbers, bell peppers, lettuce, spinach, etc.)
- 1/4 cup sliced black olives (optional)
- 1/4 cup crumbled feta cheese (optional)
- Salt and pepper, to taste

Instructions:

1. Lay out the wraps on a clean surface.
2. Spread a generous amount of hummus evenly over each wrap, leaving about an inch border around the edges.
3. Arrange the mixed vegetables on top of the hummus in the center of each wrap.
4. If using, sprinkle sliced black olives and crumbled feta cheese over the vegetables.
5. Season with salt and pepper to taste.
6. Fold the sides of the wraps inward, then roll them tightly from the bottom to form a wrap.
7. Repeat with the remaining wraps and filling ingredients.
8. If desired, cut each wrap in half diagonally before serving.

Enjoy your delicious and nutritious hummus and veggie wraps! They're perfect for a healthy lunch on the go or as a light dinner option. Feel free to customize the wraps with your favorite veggies and additional toppings.

Baked Ziti with Vegetables

Ingredients:

- 12 ounces (about 340g) ziti pasta
- 2 tablespoons olive oil
- 1 onion, finely chopped
- 2 cloves garlic, minced
- 1 bell pepper, diced
- 1 zucchini, diced
- 1 cup sliced mushrooms
- 1 (24-ounce) jar marinara sauce
- 1 teaspoon dried Italian seasoning
- Salt and pepper to taste
- 2 cups shredded mozzarella cheese
- 1/2 cup grated Parmesan cheese
- Fresh basil leaves for garnish (optional)

Instructions:

1. Preheat your oven to 375°F (190°C). Grease a 9x13-inch baking dish with olive oil or cooking spray.
2. Cook the ziti pasta according to package instructions until al dente. Drain and set aside.
3. In a large skillet, heat olive oil over medium heat. Add chopped onion and sauté until translucent, about 5 minutes. Add minced garlic and cook for another minute until fragrant.
4. Add bell pepper, zucchini, and mushrooms to the skillet. Sauté until vegetables are tender, about 5-7 minutes.
5. Stir in marinara sauce and dried Italian seasoning. Season with salt and pepper to taste. Let the mixture simmer for 5 minutes.
6. In a large bowl, combine cooked ziti pasta with the vegetable marinara sauce mixture. Stir until well combined.
7. Transfer half of the pasta mixture to the prepared baking dish. Sprinkle half of the shredded mozzarella and Parmesan cheese over the pasta.
8. Layer the remaining pasta mixture on top. Sprinkle with the remaining shredded mozzarella and Parmesan cheese.
9. Cover the baking dish with aluminum foil and bake in the preheated oven for 20 minutes.

10. Remove the foil and bake for an additional 10 minutes or until the cheese is golden and bubbly.
11. Once baked, let it cool for a few minutes before serving. Garnish with fresh basil leaves if desired.

Enjoy your delicious baked ziti with vegetables! It's a perfect comfort food for any occasion.

Egg Fried Rice

Ingredients:

- 3 cups cooked rice (preferably cooled)
- 2 tablespoons oil (vegetable or sesame oil)
- 3 eggs, lightly beaten
- 1 cup mixed vegetables (such as peas, carrots, corn, and bell peppers), diced
- 2 cloves garlic, minced
- 2 green onions, thinly sliced
- 3 tablespoons soy sauce
- Salt and pepper to taste
- Optional: 1 tablespoon oyster sauce for extra flavor

Instructions:

1. Preheat a large skillet or wok over medium-high heat. Add 1 tablespoon of oil to the skillet.
2. Pour the beaten eggs into the skillet and cook, stirring gently, until they are scrambled and cooked through. Transfer the scrambled eggs to a plate and set aside.
3. In the same skillet, add the remaining tablespoon of oil. Add minced garlic and sauté for about 30 seconds until fragrant.
4. Add the mixed vegetables to the skillet and stir-fry for 3-4 minutes until they are tender-crisp.
5. Add the cooked rice to the skillet, breaking up any clumps with a spatula. Stir-fry the rice with the vegetables for 2-3 minutes until heated through.
6. Pour the soy sauce (and oyster sauce, if using) over the rice mixture. Stir well to combine and evenly distribute the sauces.
7. Add the scrambled eggs back to the skillet. Stir-fry for another 1-2 minutes until everything is well mixed and heated through.
8. Taste the fried rice and season with salt and pepper as needed.
9. Remove the skillet from the heat. Garnish the egg fried rice with sliced green onions.
10. Serve hot as a main dish or side dish. Enjoy your homemade egg fried rice!

Feel free to customize this recipe by adding your favorite proteins like cooked chicken, shrimp, or tofu. You can also adjust the seasoning and vegetables according to your taste preferences.

Avocado Toast with Egg

Ingredients:

- 2 slices of whole grain bread (or bread of your choice)
- 1 ripe avocado
- 2 eggs
- Salt and pepper to taste
- Optional toppings: cherry tomatoes, red pepper flakes, sliced radishes, microgreens, or crumbled feta cheese

Instructions:

1. Toast the slices of bread until golden brown and crispy.
2. While the bread is toasting, cut the avocado in half and remove the pit. Scoop the avocado flesh into a bowl and mash it with a fork until smooth. Season with salt and pepper to taste.
3. Heat a non-stick skillet over medium heat. Crack the eggs into the skillet and cook them to your desired level of doneness (fried, scrambled, or poached). Season with salt and pepper.
4. Spread the mashed avocado evenly onto the toasted bread slices.
5. Place the cooked eggs on top of the mashed avocado.
6. Optional: Add your favorite toppings such as sliced cherry tomatoes, red pepper flakes, sliced radishes, microgreens, or crumbled feta cheese.
7. Season with additional salt and pepper if desired.
8. Serve immediately and enjoy your delicious avocado toast with egg!

This recipe is highly customizable, so feel free to experiment with different toppings and seasonings to suit your taste preferences. It's a satisfying and nutritious breakfast option packed with healthy fats, protein, and fiber.

Broccoli and Cheese Stuffed Baked Potatoes

Ingredients:

- 4 large baking potatoes
- 2 cups broccoli florets, chopped
- 1 tablespoon olive oil
- Salt and pepper to taste
- 1 cup shredded cheddar cheese
- 1/2 cup sour cream
- 2 green onions, thinly sliced (optional)
- Additional toppings as desired: cooked bacon bits, chopped chives, or hot sauce

Instructions:

1. Preheat your oven to 400°F (200°C). Scrub the potatoes clean and prick them several times with a fork.
2. Place the potatoes directly on the oven rack or on a baking sheet lined with aluminum foil. Bake for 45-60 minutes, or until the potatoes are tender when pierced with a fork.
3. While the potatoes are baking, steam the broccoli florets until they are tender, about 5-7 minutes. You can steam them on the stove or in the microwave.
4. Once the potatoes are done, remove them from the oven and let them cool slightly until they are safe to handle.
5. Cut each potato in half lengthwise. Carefully scoop out the insides of the potatoes into a mixing bowl, leaving a thin layer of potato inside the skins.
6. Mash the scooped-out potato with a fork or potato masher. Season with salt and pepper to taste.
7. Add the steamed broccoli and shredded cheddar cheese to the mashed potato mixture. Stir until well combined.
8. Spoon the broccoli and cheese mixture back into the potato skins, dividing it evenly among them.
9. Place the stuffed potatoes back onto the baking sheet. Return them to the oven and bake for an additional 10-15 minutes, or until the cheese is melted and bubbly.
10. Remove the stuffed potatoes from the oven and let them cool for a few minutes before serving.
11. Garnish with a dollop of sour cream, sliced green onions, and any additional toppings you like, such as cooked bacon bits, chopped chives, or hot sauce.

12. Serve the broccoli and cheese stuffed baked potatoes hot and enjoy this comforting and satisfying meal!

Feel free to customize this recipe by adding other ingredients like cooked diced chicken or ham, or by using different types of cheese according to your taste preferences.

Homemade Pizza with Tortilla Crust

Ingredients:

- Large flour tortillas (one per pizza)
- Pizza sauce
- Shredded mozzarella cheese
- Toppings of your choice (such as pepperoni, bell peppers, onions, mushrooms, olives, cooked sausage, or diced tomatoes)
- Olive oil (optional)
- Italian seasoning (optional)
- Red pepper flakes (optional)

Instructions:

1. Preheat your oven to 425°F (220°C).
2. Place a large flour tortilla on a baking sheet lined with parchment paper.
3. Spread a thin layer of pizza sauce evenly over the tortilla, leaving a small border around the edges.
4. Sprinkle shredded mozzarella cheese over the sauce, covering the entire surface of the tortilla.
5. Add your desired toppings evenly over the cheese layer. Be careful not to overload the tortilla with toppings, as it may become soggy.
6. Drizzle a small amount of olive oil over the toppings for extra flavor, if desired. Sprinkle Italian seasoning and red pepper flakes on top for added taste.
7. Place the prepared pizza in the preheated oven and bake for 8-10 minutes, or until the cheese is melted and bubbly and the edges of the tortilla are crispy.
8. Remove the pizza from the oven and let it cool for a minute or two before slicing.
9. Slice the pizza into wedges using a pizza cutter or sharp knife.
10. Serve immediately and enjoy your homemade pizza with a tortilla crust!

This recipe is versatile, allowing you to customize your pizza with your favorite toppings. It's also a great option for a quick meal or snack when you're short on time. Feel free to experiment with different sauces, cheeses, and toppings to create your perfect pizza.

Caprese Salad

Ingredients:

- 2 large ripe tomatoes, sliced into 1/4-inch rounds
- 1 ball of fresh mozzarella cheese, sliced into 1/4-inch rounds
- Fresh basil leaves
- Extra virgin olive oil
- Balsamic vinegar (optional)
- Salt and freshly ground black pepper to taste

Instructions:

1. Arrange the tomato slices and mozzarella slices alternately on a serving platter or individual plates, overlapping slightly.
2. Tuck fresh basil leaves between the tomato and mozzarella slices.
3. Drizzle extra virgin olive oil over the tomato and mozzarella slices, ensuring they are well coated.
4. Optional: If desired, drizzle a small amount of balsamic vinegar over the salad for added flavor.
5. Season the salad with a sprinkle of salt and freshly ground black pepper to taste.
6. Serve immediately as a refreshing appetizer or side dish.

Caprese salad is best enjoyed when the ingredients are fresh and at room temperature.

It's a simple yet elegant dish that is perfect for showcasing the flavors of summer produce. Enjoy!

Grilled Cheese Sandwiches

Ingredients:

- 4 slices of bread (white, whole wheat, or sourdough)
- Butter or margarine, softened
- 2 cups shredded cheese (cheddar, mozzarella, Swiss, or your favorite cheese)
- Optional: Sliced tomato, cooked bacon, ham, or avocado

Instructions:

1. Preheat a skillet or griddle over medium heat.
2. Butter one side of each slice of bread.
3. Place two slices of bread, buttered side down, onto the skillet or griddle.
4. Sprinkle shredded cheese evenly over the bread slices on the skillet.
5. If using, add any optional toppings such as sliced tomato, cooked bacon, ham, or avocado on top of the cheese.
6. Top each sandwich with the remaining slices of bread, buttered side facing up.
7. Cook the sandwiches for 3-4 minutes on each side, or until the bread is golden brown and crispy, and the cheese is melted.
8. Carefully flip the sandwiches using a spatula, and continue to cook until the other side is golden brown and the cheese is melted.
9. Remove the sandwiches from the skillet and let them cool for a minute before slicing.
10. Slice the sandwiches diagonally and serve hot.

Grilled cheese sandwiches are perfect for dipping into tomato soup or enjoying on their own as a quick and comforting meal. Feel free to get creative with your cheese and toppings to customize your sandwiches to your taste preferences!

Veggie Omelette

Ingredients:

- 3 large eggs
- 1/4 cup diced bell peppers (any color)
- 1/4 cup diced onions
- 1/4 cup diced tomatoes
- 1/4 cup chopped spinach or kale
- Salt and pepper to taste
- 1 tablespoon olive oil or butter
- Optional: Grated cheese (such as cheddar, mozzarella, or feta)
- Optional: Chopped herbs (such as parsley, chives, or cilantro)

Instructions:

1. Prepare the vegetables by dicing the bell peppers, onions, and tomatoes, and chopping the spinach or kale.
2. In a bowl, crack the eggs and beat them lightly with a fork or whisk. Season with salt and pepper to taste.
3. Heat olive oil or butter in a non-stick skillet over medium heat.
4. Add the diced bell peppers and onions to the skillet. Cook, stirring occasionally, until they are softened and slightly caramelized, about 3-4 minutes.
5. Add the diced tomatoes and chopped spinach or kale to the skillet. Cook for an additional 1-2 minutes until the spinach wilts and the tomatoes soften slightly.
6. Pour the beaten eggs evenly over the cooked vegetables in the skillet.
7. Let the eggs cook undisturbed for a minute or two until the edges start to set.
8. Using a spatula, gently lift the edges of the omelette and tilt the skillet to allow the uncooked eggs to flow underneath.
9. Continue cooking the omelette until the eggs are mostly set but still slightly runny on top.
10. If using, sprinkle grated cheese over one half of the omelette.
11. Fold the other half of the omelette over the cheese to create a half-moon shape.
12. Cook for another 1-2 minutes until the cheese melts and the omelette is cooked through.
13. Slide the omelette onto a plate and garnish with chopped herbs if desired.
14. Serve hot and enjoy your delicious veggie omelette!

Feel free to customize your veggie omelette with your favorite vegetables, cheese, and herbs. It's a versatile dish that's perfect for breakfast, brunch, or even a light dinner.

Pasta with Marinara Sauce

Ingredients:

- 8 ounces (about 225 grams) of your favorite pasta (such as spaghetti, penne, or fettuccine)
- 2 tablespoons olive oil
- 3 cloves garlic, minced
- 1 (24-ounce) jar of marinara sauce (or homemade marinara sauce)
- Salt and pepper to taste
- Fresh basil leaves, chopped (optional)
- Grated Parmesan cheese for serving (optional)

Instructions:

1. Cook the pasta according to the package instructions until al dente. Drain the pasta and set it aside, reserving some of the pasta water.
2. In a large skillet, heat the olive oil over medium heat. Add the minced garlic and sauté for 1-2 minutes until fragrant, being careful not to burn it.
3. Pour the marinara sauce into the skillet with the garlic. Stir well to combine and heat the sauce until it starts to simmer.
4. Season the marinara sauce with salt and pepper to taste. You can also add a pinch of sugar if the sauce is too acidic.
5. Add the cooked pasta to the skillet with the marinara sauce. Toss well to coat the pasta evenly with the sauce. If the sauce is too thick, you can add a splash of reserved pasta water to loosen it.
6. Continue cooking the pasta in the sauce for 1-2 minutes, stirring occasionally, until the pasta is heated through.
7. Optional: Stir in chopped fresh basil leaves for extra flavor and freshness.
8. Remove the skillet from the heat and serve the pasta with marinara sauce hot.
9. Garnish with grated Parmesan cheese if desired.
10. Enjoy your delicious pasta with marinara sauce as a simple and satisfying meal!

Feel free to customize this recipe by adding your favorite ingredients such as cooked meatballs, grilled chicken, sautéed vegetables, or crushed red pepper flakes for a spicy kick.

Oatmeal with Fruit and Nuts

Ingredients:

- 1/2 cup rolled oats
- 1 cup water or milk (dairy or plant-based)
- Pinch of salt
- 1/2 banana, sliced
- 1/4 cup fresh berries (such as strawberries, blueberries, or raspberries)
- 1 tablespoon chopped nuts (such as almonds, walnuts, or pecans)
- Optional toppings: honey, maple syrup, cinnamon, chia seeds, or shredded coconut

Instructions:

1. In a small saucepan, bring the water or milk to a boil over medium heat.
2. Stir in the rolled oats and a pinch of salt. Reduce the heat to low and simmer, stirring occasionally, for 5-7 minutes or until the oats are cooked and the mixture has thickened to your desired consistency.
3. Once the oatmeal is cooked, remove it from the heat and transfer it to a serving bowl.
4. Top the oatmeal with sliced banana, fresh berries, and chopped nuts.
5. Drizzle with honey or maple syrup for added sweetness if desired.
6. Sprinkle with cinnamon, chia seeds, or shredded coconut for extra flavor and texture.
7. Serve immediately and enjoy your delicious oatmeal with fruit and nuts!

Feel free to customize this recipe by using different types of fruit and nuts according to your taste preferences. You can also add other toppings such as dried fruit, yogurt, or nut butter for additional variety and nutrition. Oatmeal with fruit and nuts is a versatile breakfast dish that's perfect for fueling your day with wholesome goodness.

Tofu Stir-Fry with Noodles

Ingredients:

- 8 ounces (about 225 grams) of firm tofu, drained and pressed
- 8 ounces (about 225 grams) of noodles (such as udon, soba, or rice noodles)
- 2 tablespoons soy sauce
- 1 tablespoon hoisin sauce
- 1 tablespoon sesame oil
- 2 cloves garlic, minced
- 1 tablespoon ginger, minced
- 1 bell pepper, sliced
- 1 carrot, julienned
- 1 cup broccoli florets
- 1/2 cup sliced mushrooms
- 2 green onions, sliced
- 2 tablespoons vegetable oil
- Sesame seeds and chopped cilantro for garnish (optional)

Instructions:

1. Prepare the tofu by draining it and pressing out excess moisture. Cut the tofu into cubes or strips and set aside.
2. Cook the noodles according to the package instructions until al dente. Drain and rinse the noodles under cold water to stop the cooking process. Set aside.
3. In a small bowl, whisk together the soy sauce, hoisin sauce, and sesame oil to make the sauce. Set aside.
4. Heat 1 tablespoon of vegetable oil in a large skillet or wok over medium-high heat.
5. Add the tofu cubes to the skillet in a single layer. Cook for 3-4 minutes on each side until golden brown and crispy. Remove the tofu from the skillet and set aside.
6. In the same skillet, add the remaining tablespoon of vegetable oil. Add the minced garlic and ginger, and cook for 1 minute until fragrant.
7. Add the sliced bell pepper, julienned carrot, broccoli florets, and sliced mushrooms to the skillet. Stir-fry for 5-6 minutes until the vegetables are tender-crisp.
8. Return the cooked tofu to the skillet with the vegetables.
9. Pour the sauce over the tofu and vegetables in the skillet. Stir well to coat everything evenly with the sauce.

10. Add the cooked noodles to the skillet and toss gently to combine with the tofu and vegetables.
11. Cook for an additional 2-3 minutes, stirring occasionally, until everything is heated through.
12. Remove the skillet from the heat and garnish with sliced green onions, sesame seeds, and chopped cilantro if desired.
13. Serve immediately and enjoy your delicious tofu stir-fry with noodles!

Feel free to customize this recipe by adding your favorite vegetables or adjusting the sauce to your taste preferences. It's a versatile and satisfying dish that's perfect for a quick and healthy meal.

Black Bean Soup

Ingredients:

- 2 tablespoons olive oil
- 1 onion, chopped
- 2 cloves garlic, minced
- 2 carrots, diced
- 2 stalks celery, diced
- 2 cans (15 ounces each) black beans, drained and rinsed
- 4 cups vegetable or chicken broth
- 1 teaspoon ground cumin
- 1 teaspoon chili powder
- 1/2 teaspoon smoked paprika
- Salt and pepper to taste
- Juice of 1 lime
- Optional toppings: chopped cilantro, diced avocado, sour cream, shredded cheese, or tortilla strips

Instructions:

1. Heat olive oil in a large pot or Dutch oven over medium heat.
2. Add the chopped onion, minced garlic, diced carrots, and diced celery to the pot. Cook, stirring occasionally, for 5-7 minutes until the vegetables are softened.
3. Stir in the drained and rinsed black beans, vegetable or chicken broth, ground cumin, chili powder, and smoked paprika.
4. Bring the soup to a simmer, then reduce the heat to low. Cover the pot and let the soup simmer for 15-20 minutes to allow the flavors to meld together.
5. Using an immersion blender or regular blender, blend the soup until smooth and creamy. Alternatively, you can leave some of the soup chunky if you prefer a textured soup.
6. Season the soup with salt and pepper to taste. Stir in the lime juice for a bright, citrusy flavor.
7. Taste and adjust the seasoning if needed.
8. Serve the black bean soup hot, garnished with chopped cilantro, diced avocado, sour cream, shredded cheese, or tortilla strips if desired.
9. Enjoy your delicious and comforting black bean soup!

This soup can be stored in the refrigerator for up to 4 days or frozen for longer storage. It's a versatile dish that's perfect for lunch, dinner, or meal prep for the week.

Couscous Salad with Chickpeas and Veggies

Ingredients:

- 1 cup couscous
- 1 1/4 cups vegetable broth or water
- 1 can (15 ounces) chickpeas, drained and rinsed
- 1 cup cherry tomatoes, halved
- 1 cucumber, diced
- 1 bell pepper, diced
- 1/4 cup red onion, finely chopped
- 1/4 cup fresh parsley, chopped
- 1/4 cup fresh mint leaves, chopped
- 1/4 cup crumbled feta cheese (optional)
- Juice of 1 lemon
- 2 tablespoons extra virgin olive oil
- Salt and pepper to taste

Instructions:

1. Prepare the couscous according to the package instructions. In a saucepan, bring the vegetable broth or water to a boil. Stir in the couscous, cover, and remove from heat. Let it sit for 5 minutes, then fluff with a fork.
2. In a large bowl, combine the cooked couscous, chickpeas, cherry tomatoes, cucumber, bell pepper, red onion, parsley, and mint leaves.
3. Add the crumbled feta cheese to the salad if using.
4. In a small bowl, whisk together the lemon juice and extra virgin olive oil to make the dressing.
5. Pour the dressing over the couscous salad and toss gently to coat everything evenly.
6. Season the salad with salt and pepper to taste.
7. Cover the salad and refrigerate for at least 30 minutes to allow the flavors to meld together.
8. Before serving, taste the salad and adjust the seasoning if needed. You can also garnish with additional fresh herbs if desired.
9. Serve the couscous salad with chickpeas and veggies as a light and refreshing meal or side dish.
10. Enjoy your delicious and nutritious couscous salad with chickpeas and veggies!

Feel free to customize this recipe by adding other vegetables or herbs according to your taste preferences. You can also substitute the feta cheese with other types of cheese or omit it altogether for a vegan version of the salad.

Mexican Rice and Beans

Ingredients:

- 1 cup long-grain white rice
- 1 tablespoon vegetable oil
- 1 small onion, diced
- 2 cloves garlic, minced
- 1 teaspoon ground cumin
- 1 teaspoon chili powder
- 1/2 teaspoon paprika
- 1 can (15 ounces) black beans, drained and rinsed
- 1 can (14.5 ounces) diced tomatoes, undrained
- 1 3/4 cups vegetable broth or water
- Salt and pepper to taste
- Fresh cilantro, chopped (for garnish, optional)
- Lime wedges (for serving, optional)

Instructions:

1. Rinse the rice under cold water until the water runs clear. Drain well and set aside.
2. Heat the vegetable oil in a large skillet or saucepan over medium heat.
3. Add the diced onion to the skillet and cook for 3-4 minutes until softened.
4. Stir in the minced garlic, ground cumin, chili powder, and paprika. Cook for another 1-2 minutes until fragrant.
5. Add the rinsed rice to the skillet and cook, stirring frequently, for 2-3 minutes until the rice is lightly toasted.
6. Pour in the diced tomatoes (with their juices), black beans, and vegetable broth or water. Stir well to combine.
7. Bring the mixture to a boil, then reduce the heat to low. Cover the skillet and simmer for 15-20 minutes, or until the rice is tender and the liquid is absorbed. Stir occasionally to prevent sticking.
8. Once the rice is cooked, remove the skillet from the heat. Season with salt and pepper to taste, and fluff the rice with a fork.
9. Garnish the Mexican rice and beans with chopped cilantro, if desired.
10. Serve hot, with lime wedges on the side for squeezing over the dish if desired.
11. Enjoy your delicious homemade Mexican rice and beans!

This dish is versatile and can be customized with your favorite toppings such as avocado slices, sour cream, or shredded cheese. It's perfect for a satisfying weeknight meal or for feeding a crowd at your next gathering.

Spinach and Feta Quesadillas

Ingredients:

- 4 large flour tortillas
- 2 cups fresh spinach leaves, chopped
- 1 cup crumbled feta cheese
- 1/2 cup shredded mozzarella cheese
- 1/4 cup diced red onion
- 2 cloves garlic, minced
- 1 tablespoon olive oil
- Salt and pepper to taste
- Optional: Sliced cherry tomatoes, sliced black olives, chopped bell peppers, or cooked chicken

Instructions:

1. Prepare the filling: In a skillet, heat olive oil over medium heat. Add minced garlic and diced red onion, and sauté for 2-3 minutes until softened.
2. Add chopped spinach leaves to the skillet and cook until wilted, about 1-2 minutes. Season with salt and pepper to taste. Remove from heat and let it cool slightly.
3. In a mixing bowl, combine the cooked spinach mixture with crumbled feta cheese and shredded mozzarella cheese. Mix well to combine.
4. Place one flour tortilla on a flat surface. Spread an even layer of the spinach and feta mixture over half of the tortilla, leaving a small border around the edges.
5. Optional: Add any additional toppings such as sliced cherry tomatoes, sliced black olives, chopped bell peppers, or cooked chicken on top of the spinach and feta mixture.
6. Fold the other half of the tortilla over the filling to form a half-moon shape.
7. Repeat the process with the remaining tortillas and filling mixture.
8. Heat a large skillet or griddle over medium heat. Place the assembled quesadillas in the skillet and cook for 2-3 minutes on each side, or until golden brown and crispy, and the cheese is melted.
9. Remove the quesadillas from the skillet and let them cool for a minute before slicing into wedges.
10. Serve the spinach and feta quesadillas hot, with your favorite dipping sauce or salsa on the side.
11. Enjoy your delicious spinach and feta quesadillas as a quick and satisfying meal or snack!

Feel free to customize this recipe by adding or substituting ingredients according to your taste preferences. You can also serve these quesadillas with a side of guacamole, sour cream, or salsa for dipping.

Baked Chicken Drumsticks

Ingredients:

- 8 chicken drumsticks
- 2 tablespoons olive oil
- 2 cloves garlic, minced
- 1 teaspoon paprika
- 1 teaspoon dried thyme
- 1 teaspoon dried oregano
- 1 teaspoon onion powder
- 1/2 teaspoon salt
- 1/4 teaspoon black pepper
- Lemon wedges for serving (optional)
- Chopped fresh parsley for garnish (optional)

Instructions:

1. Preheat your oven to 425°F (220°C). Line a baking sheet with aluminum foil or parchment paper for easy cleanup.
2. In a small bowl, combine the olive oil, minced garlic, paprika, dried thyme, dried oregano, onion powder, salt, and black pepper. Mix well to form a marinade.
3. Pat the chicken drumsticks dry with paper towels. Place them in a large mixing bowl or a resealable plastic bag.
4. Pour the marinade over the chicken drumsticks, making sure they are evenly coated. Use your hands to massage the marinade into the chicken.
5. Arrange the chicken drumsticks in a single layer on the prepared baking sheet.
6. Bake in the preheated oven for 35-40 minutes, or until the chicken is cooked through and the skin is crispy and golden brown. You can check for doneness by inserting a meat thermometer into the thickest part of the drumstick; it should register at least 165°F (74°C).
7. Once done, remove the chicken drumsticks from the oven and let them rest for a few minutes before serving.
8. Optional: Garnish with chopped fresh parsley and serve with lemon wedges on the side for squeezing over the chicken.
9. Enjoy your delicious baked chicken drumsticks as a main course, accompanied by your favorite sides such as roasted vegetables, mashed potatoes, or a fresh salad.

Feel free to customize this recipe by adjusting the seasonings according to your taste preferences. You can also add other herbs and spices such as rosemary, sage, or chili powder for extra flavor.

Pancakes with Maple Syrup

Ingredients:

- 1 cup all-purpose flour
- 2 tablespoons granulated sugar
- 1 teaspoon baking powder
- 1/2 teaspoon baking soda
- 1/4 teaspoon salt
- 1 cup buttermilk (or 1 cup milk mixed with 1 tablespoon lemon juice or vinegar)
- 1 large egg
- 2 tablespoons unsalted butter, melted
- Maple syrup, for serving
- Optional toppings: Fresh berries, sliced bananas, chopped nuts, or whipped cream

Instructions:

1. In a large mixing bowl, whisk together the flour, sugar, baking powder, baking soda, and salt until well combined.
2. In a separate bowl, whisk together the buttermilk, egg, and melted butter until smooth.
3. Pour the wet ingredients into the dry ingredients and stir until just combined. Be careful not to overmix; a few lumps in the batter are okay.
4. Preheat a non-stick skillet or griddle over medium heat. Lightly grease the skillet with butter or cooking spray.
5. Pour about 1/4 cup of pancake batter onto the skillet for each pancake, using a ladle or measuring cup to ensure even portions.
6. Cook the pancakes for 2-3 minutes, or until bubbles form on the surface and the edges start to look set.
7. Flip the pancakes and cook for an additional 1-2 minutes on the other side, or until golden brown and cooked through.
8. Transfer the cooked pancakes to a plate and keep warm while you cook the remaining batter.
9. Serve the pancakes hot, topped with maple syrup and any optional toppings of your choice.
10. Enjoy your delicious pancakes with maple syrup for a comforting and satisfying breakfast!

Feel free to customize this recipe by adding chocolate chips, blueberries, or sliced bananas to the pancake batter for extra flavor and texture. You can also make a larger batch of pancakes and freeze the leftovers for a quick and convenient breakfast on busy mornings.

Tomato and Mozzarella Panini

Ingredients:

- 4 slices of bread (such as ciabatta, sourdough, or Italian bread)
- 1 large tomato, thinly sliced
- 8 ounces (about 225 grams) fresh mozzarella cheese, thinly sliced
- 2 tablespoons basil pesto
- 2 tablespoons olive oil or melted butter

Instructions:

1. Preheat a panini press or grill pan over medium heat.
2. Spread basil pesto evenly on one side of each slice of bread.
3. Layer the tomato slices and mozzarella cheese on top of the pesto-covered side of two bread slices.
4. Place the remaining two bread slices on top to form sandwiches, with the pesto side facing inward.
5. Brush the outer sides of the sandwiches with olive oil or melted butter.
6. Place the sandwiches on the preheated panini press or grill pan.
7. Cook the sandwiches for 3-4 minutes, or until the bread is golden brown and crispy, and the cheese is melted.
8. Carefully remove the sandwiches from the panini press or grill pan and let them cool for a minute before slicing.
9. Slice the tomato and mozzarella panini in half diagonally and serve hot.
10. Enjoy your delicious and cheesy tomato and mozzarella panini!

Feel free to customize this recipe by adding additional ingredients such as sliced cooked chicken, prosciutto, roasted red peppers, or fresh spinach. Serve the panini with a side of mixed greens or tomato soup for a complete meal.

Pita Bread Pizzas

Ingredients:

- 4 large pita bread rounds
- 1 cup pizza sauce
- 2 cups shredded mozzarella cheese
- Your favorite pizza toppings (such as sliced pepperoni, diced bell peppers, sliced mushrooms, sliced olives, etc.)
- Olive oil (for brushing)

Instructions:

1. Preheat your oven to 400°F (200°C). Line a baking sheet with parchment paper or aluminum foil for easy cleanup.
2. Place the pita bread rounds on the prepared baking sheet.
3. Spread a thin layer of pizza sauce evenly over each pita bread round, leaving a small border around the edges.
4. Sprinkle shredded mozzarella cheese over the sauce on each pita bread round.
5. Add your favorite pizza toppings on top of the cheese. Get creative and customize each pita bread pizza to your liking!
6. Lightly brush the edges of the pita bread rounds with olive oil to help them crisp up in the oven.
7. Bake the pita bread pizzas in the preheated oven for 8-10 minutes, or until the cheese is melted and bubbly, and the edges of the pita bread are golden brown and crispy.
8. Remove the pita bread pizzas from the oven and let them cool for a minute before slicing.
9. Slice the pita bread pizzas into wedges or squares and serve hot.
10. Enjoy your delicious and easy homemade pita bread pizzas!

Feel free to experiment with different toppings and sauces to create your favorite flavor combinations. Pita bread pizzas are perfect for a quick lunch, dinner, or snack, and they're also great for serving at parties or gatherings.

Creamy Mushroom Risotto

Ingredients:

- 1 1/2 cups Arborio rice
- 4 cups vegetable or chicken broth
- 2 tablespoons olive oil
- 1 tablespoon unsalted butter
- 1 onion, finely chopped
- 2 cloves garlic, minced
- 8 ounces (about 225 grams) mushrooms (such as cremini or button), sliced
- 1/2 cup dry white wine (optional)
- 1/2 cup grated Parmesan cheese
- Salt and pepper to taste
- Chopped fresh parsley for garnish (optional)

Instructions:

1. In a medium saucepan, heat the vegetable or chicken broth over low heat. Keep it warm while you prepare the risotto.
2. In a large skillet or Dutch oven, heat the olive oil and butter over medium heat.
3. Add the chopped onion to the skillet and cook, stirring occasionally, for 3-4 minutes until softened.
4. Stir in the minced garlic and cook for an additional 1-2 minutes until fragrant.
5. Add the sliced mushrooms to the skillet and cook, stirring occasionally, for 5-6 minutes until they are browned and tender.
6. Add the Arborio rice to the skillet and stir to coat it with the oil and butter, allowing it to toast slightly for 1-2 minutes.
7. Optional: Pour in the dry white wine and cook, stirring constantly, until it is absorbed by the rice.
8. Begin adding the warm broth to the skillet, one ladleful at a time, stirring constantly and allowing each addition of broth to be absorbed before adding more. This process will take about 20-25 minutes until the rice is creamy and cooked al dente.
9. Once the risotto is cooked, stir in the grated Parmesan cheese until it is melted and well incorporated.
10. Season the risotto with salt and pepper to taste.
11. Garnish the creamy mushroom risotto with chopped fresh parsley, if desired.
12. Serve the risotto hot, and enjoy its creamy and flavorful goodness!

Creamy mushroom risotto is a versatile dish that can be served as a main course or as a side dish alongside grilled meats or roasted vegetables. It's perfect for special occasions or for a comforting meal any day of the week.

Banana Bread

Ingredients:

- 2-3 ripe bananas, mashed (about 1 cup)
- 1/2 cup unsalted butter, melted
- 1/2 cup granulated sugar
- 1/2 cup brown sugar, packed
- 2 large eggs
- 1 teaspoon vanilla extract
- 1 1/2 cups all-purpose flour
- 1 teaspoon baking soda
- 1/2 teaspoon salt
- Optional add-ins: chopped nuts (such as walnuts or pecans), chocolate chips, or dried fruit

Instructions:

1. Preheat your oven to 350°F (175°C). Grease a 9x5-inch loaf pan or line it with parchment paper for easy removal.
2. In a large mixing bowl, mash the ripe bananas with a fork or potato masher until smooth.
3. Add the melted butter, granulated sugar, brown sugar, eggs, and vanilla extract to the mashed bananas. Stir until well combined.
4. In a separate bowl, whisk together the all-purpose flour, baking soda, and salt.
5. Gradually add the dry ingredients to the wet ingredients, stirring until just combined. Be careful not to overmix; a few lumps in the batter are okay.
6. If using, fold in any optional add-ins such as chopped nuts, chocolate chips, or dried fruit.
7. Pour the batter into the prepared loaf pan, spreading it out evenly with a spatula.
8. Bake in the preheated oven for 50-60 minutes, or until a toothpick inserted into the center of the bread comes out clean.
9. Once done, remove the banana bread from the oven and let it cool in the pan for 10-15 minutes.
10. Carefully transfer the banana bread to a wire rack to cool completely before slicing.
11. Slice the banana bread into thick slices and serve warm or at room temperature.
12. Enjoy your delicious homemade banana bread as a snack, breakfast, or dessert!

Feel free to customize this recipe by adding your favorite mix-ins or toppings. You can also wrap the cooled banana bread tightly in plastic wrap or aluminum foil and store it at room temperature for up to 3 days, or in the refrigerator for up to a week. It also freezes well for longer storage.

Corn and Black Bean Salad

Ingredients:

- 2 cups cooked corn kernels (fresh, canned, or frozen and thawed)
- 1 can (15 ounces) black beans, drained and rinsed
- 1 red bell pepper, diced
- 1/2 red onion, finely chopped
- 1/4 cup chopped fresh cilantro
- 2 tablespoons olive oil
- 2 tablespoons lime juice
- 1 teaspoon ground cumin
- 1/2 teaspoon chili powder
- Salt and pepper to taste
- Optional add-ins: diced avocado, diced tomatoes, chopped green onions, or crumbled feta cheese

Instructions:

1. In a large mixing bowl, combine the cooked corn kernels, black beans, diced red bell pepper, finely chopped red onion, and chopped fresh cilantro.
2. In a small bowl, whisk together the olive oil, lime juice, ground cumin, chili powder, salt, and pepper to make the dressing.
3. Pour the dressing over the corn and black bean mixture in the large bowl.
4. Toss gently to coat all the ingredients evenly with the dressing.
5. If using, add any optional add-ins such as diced avocado, diced tomatoes, chopped green onions, or crumbled feta cheese. Gently toss again to combine.
6. Cover the bowl with plastic wrap or a lid and refrigerate for at least 30 minutes to allow the flavors to meld together.
7. Before serving, give the salad a final toss and taste for seasoning, adding more salt and pepper if needed.
8. Transfer the corn and black bean salad to a serving bowl or platter.
9. Garnish with additional chopped cilantro or lime wedges if desired.
10. Serve the salad chilled or at room temperature as a side dish or appetizer.
11. Enjoy your delicious and nutritious corn and black bean salad!

This salad is versatile and can be customized to suit your taste preferences. Feel free to

adjust the seasonings or add other ingredients such as diced jalapeños for extra heat, or grilled corn for a smoky flavor. It's a colorful and flavorful dish that's sure to be a hit at any gathering.

Vegetable Frittata

Ingredients:

- 8 large eggs
- 1/4 cup milk or heavy cream
- Salt and pepper to taste
- 2 tablespoons olive oil or butter
- 1 small onion, diced
- 1 bell pepper, diced
- 1 cup sliced mushrooms
- 1 cup baby spinach leaves
- 1/2 cup cherry tomatoes, halved
- 1/2 cup shredded cheese (such as cheddar, mozzarella, or feta)
- Optional add-ins: diced zucchini, diced potatoes, cooked bacon or sausage, or fresh herbs

Instructions:

1. Preheat your oven to 375°F (190°C). Grease a 10-inch oven-safe skillet or pie dish with cooking spray or butter.
2. In a large mixing bowl, whisk together the eggs, milk or heavy cream, salt, and pepper until well combined. Set aside.
3. Heat olive oil or butter in the skillet over medium heat.
4. Add the diced onion and cook for 2-3 minutes until softened.
5. Stir in the diced bell pepper and sliced mushrooms, and cook for an additional 3-4 minutes until the vegetables are tender.
6. Add the baby spinach leaves and cherry tomatoes to the skillet, and cook for 1-2 minutes until the spinach is wilted.
7. Spread the cooked vegetables evenly in the skillet.
8. Pour the egg mixture over the vegetables in the skillet.
9. Sprinkle the shredded cheese evenly over the top of the frittata.
10. If using, add any optional add-ins such as diced zucchini, diced potatoes, cooked bacon or sausage, or fresh herbs.
11. Transfer the skillet to the preheated oven and bake for 20-25 minutes, or until the frittata is set in the center and the edges are golden brown.
12. Once done, remove the skillet from the oven and let the frittata cool for a few minutes before slicing.
13. Slice the vegetable frittata into wedges and serve hot or at room temperature.
14. Enjoy your delicious and hearty vegetable frittata!

This vegetable frittata is a great way to use up leftover vegetables and customize it with your favorite ingredients. It's perfect for meal prep and can be enjoyed for breakfast, brunch, lunch, or dinner.

Potato and Pea Curry

Ingredients:

- 3 medium potatoes, peeled and diced
- 1 cup frozen peas, thawed
- 1 onion, finely chopped
- 2 cloves garlic, minced
- 1-inch piece of ginger, grated
- 2 tomatoes, finely chopped (or 1 can of diced tomatoes)
- 1 green chili pepper, finely chopped (optional, for heat)
- 1 teaspoon cumin seeds
- 1 teaspoon ground turmeric
- 1 teaspoon ground coriander
- 1/2 teaspoon ground cumin
- 1/2 teaspoon red chili powder (adjust to taste)
- 1 teaspoon garam masala
- Salt to taste
- 2 tablespoons vegetable oil
- Fresh cilantro leaves for garnish (optional)

Instructions:

1. Heat the vegetable oil in a large skillet or pot over medium heat.
2. Add the cumin seeds to the hot oil and let them sizzle for a few seconds until fragrant.
3. Add the chopped onion to the skillet and cook, stirring occasionally, until it becomes soft and translucent.
4. Stir in the minced garlic and grated ginger, and cook for another minute until fragrant.
5. Add the diced potatoes to the skillet and cook for 5-7 minutes, stirring occasionally, until they start to soften slightly.
6. Stir in the chopped tomatoes and green chili pepper (if using), and cook for another 3-4 minutes until the tomatoes break down and become pulpy.
7. Add the ground turmeric, ground coriander, ground cumin, red chili powder, and salt to the skillet, and stir well to coat the ingredients with the spices.
8. Pour in about 1/2 to 1 cup of water to the skillet, enough to cover the potatoes. Bring the mixture to a simmer.
9. Cover the skillet and let the potato mixture cook for 10-12 minutes, or until the potatoes are tender and cooked through.

10. Once the potatoes are cooked, add the thawed peas to the skillet and stir well to combine.
11. Cook for an additional 3-4 minutes, or until the peas are heated through.
12. Stir in the garam masala and adjust the seasoning with salt if needed.
13. Garnish the potato and pea curry with fresh cilantro leaves, if desired.
14. Serve the potato and pea curry hot, with steamed rice or warm naan bread.
15. Enjoy your delicious and comforting potato and pea curry!

This potato and pea curry is rich in flavor and can be easily customized by adjusting the spices and adding other vegetables or protein sources such as tofu or chickpeas. It's a satisfying dish that's perfect for a weeknight dinner or for entertaining guests.

Egg Salad Sandwiches

Ingredients:

- 6 large eggs
- 1/4 cup mayonnaise
- 1 tablespoon Dijon mustard
- 1 tablespoon lemon juice
- 2 tablespoons finely chopped red onion
- 2 tablespoons finely chopped celery
- 1 tablespoon finely chopped fresh parsley
- Salt and pepper to taste
- 8 slices of bread (such as whole wheat, white, or sourdough)
- Lettuce leaves and/or sliced tomatoes for serving (optional)

Instructions:

1. Hard-boil the eggs: Place the eggs in a saucepan and cover them with water. Bring the water to a boil over medium-high heat, then reduce the heat to low and simmer for 10-12 minutes. Remove the eggs from the water and place them in a bowl of ice water to cool completely. Once cooled, peel the eggs and chop them into small pieces.
2. In a large mixing bowl, combine the chopped hard-boiled eggs, mayonnaise, Dijon mustard, lemon juice, finely chopped red onion, finely chopped celery, and finely chopped fresh parsley. Mix well to combine.
3. Season the egg salad with salt and pepper to taste, adjusting the seasoning as needed.
4. Toast the slices of bread, if desired.
5. Spread a generous amount of the egg salad mixture onto one slice of bread.
6. If using, top the egg salad with lettuce leaves and/or sliced tomatoes for extra freshness and crunch.
7. Place another slice of bread on top to form a sandwich.
8. Repeat with the remaining slices of bread and egg salad mixture to make additional sandwiches.
9. Slice each sandwich in half diagonally, if desired.
10. Serve the egg salad sandwiches immediately, or wrap them tightly in plastic wrap and refrigerate until ready to serve.
11. Enjoy your delicious and satisfying egg salad sandwiches!

Feel free to customize this recipe by adding other ingredients such as chopped pickles, diced bell peppers, or sliced avocado. You can also use different types of bread or serve the egg salad on a bed of lettuce for a lighter option.

Stuffed Bell Peppers

Ingredients:

- 4 large bell peppers (any color), halved and seeds removed
- 1 cup cooked rice (white or brown)
- 1 pound ground beef or turkey (or substitute with cooked lentils for a vegetarian option)
- 1 small onion, finely chopped
- 2 cloves garlic, minced
- 1 can (14.5 ounces) diced tomatoes, drained
- 1 cup shredded cheese (such as cheddar or mozzarella)
- 1 teaspoon dried oregano
- 1 teaspoon dried basil
- Salt and pepper to taste
- Olive oil for cooking
- Chopped fresh parsley for garnish (optional)

Instructions:

1. Preheat your oven to 375°F (190°C). Grease a baking dish large enough to hold the halved bell peppers.
2. In a large skillet, heat olive oil over medium heat. Add the chopped onion and minced garlic, and cook until softened, about 2-3 minutes.
3. Add the ground beef or turkey to the skillet, and cook until browned and cooked through, breaking it up with a spoon as it cooks.
4. Once the meat is cooked, drain any excess fat from the skillet.
5. Stir in the cooked rice, diced tomatoes, dried oregano, and dried basil. Season with salt and pepper to taste. Cook for another 2-3 minutes to allow the flavors to meld together.
6. Remove the skillet from heat and let the mixture cool slightly.
7. Place the halved bell peppers, cut side up, in the prepared baking dish.
8. Spoon the meat and rice mixture into each bell pepper half, filling them to the top.
9. Sprinkle shredded cheese over the top of each stuffed bell pepper.
10. Cover the baking dish with aluminum foil and bake in the preheated oven for 25-30 minutes, or until the bell peppers are tender and the cheese is melted and bubbly.
11. Once done, remove the foil and bake for an additional 5-10 minutes to brown the cheese slightly.

12. Remove the stuffed bell peppers from the oven and let them cool for a few minutes before serving.
13. Garnish with chopped fresh parsley, if desired, before serving.
14. Serve the stuffed bell peppers hot as a satisfying and flavorful meal.

Feel free to customize this recipe by adding other ingredients such as black beans, corn, diced tomatoes, or quinoa to the filling mixture. You can also experiment with different cheeses or seasonings to suit your taste preferences. Enjoy your delicious stuffed bell peppers!

Tuna Melt Sandwiches

Ingredients:

- 2 cans (5 ounces each) tuna, drained
- 1/4 cup mayonnaise
- 2 tablespoons finely chopped red onion
- 2 tablespoons finely chopped celery
- 1 tablespoon lemon juice
- 1/2 teaspoon Dijon mustard
- Salt and pepper to taste
- 4 slices of bread (such as whole wheat, white, or sourdough)
- 4 slices of cheese (such as cheddar, Swiss, or provolone)
- Butter or margarine for spreading

Instructions:

1. In a medium mixing bowl, combine the drained tuna, mayonnaise, finely chopped red onion, finely chopped celery, lemon juice, Dijon mustard, salt, and pepper. Mix well to combine.
2. Spread butter or margarine on one side of each slice of bread.
3. Divide the tuna mixture evenly among two slices of bread, spreading it out to cover the entire slice.
4. Top each slice of tuna-covered bread with a slice of cheese.
5. Place the remaining slices of bread on top to form sandwiches, with the buttered side facing outward.
6. Preheat a skillet or griddle over medium heat.
7. Place the sandwiches in the skillet and cook for 3-4 minutes on each side, or until the bread is golden brown and crispy, and the cheese is melted.
8. Once done, remove the sandwiches from the skillet and let them cool for a minute before slicing.
9. Slice the tuna melt sandwiches in half diagonally, if desired.
10. Serve the tuna melt sandwiches hot, with your favorite sides such as potato chips, coleslaw, or a side salad.
11. Enjoy your delicious and cheesy tuna melt sandwiches!

Feel free to customize this recipe by adding other ingredients such as sliced tomatoes, avocado, or pickles to the tuna mixture for extra flavor and texture. You can also experiment with different types of bread or cheese to suit your taste preferences.

Three Bean Chili

Ingredients:

- 1 tablespoon olive oil
- 1 onion, chopped
- 2 cloves garlic, minced
- 1 bell pepper, chopped (any color)
- 1 can (15 ounces) black beans, drained and rinsed
- 1 can (15 ounces) kidney beans, drained and rinsed
- 1 can (15 ounces) pinto beans, drained and rinsed
- 1 can (14.5 ounces) diced tomatoes
- 1 cup vegetable broth or water
- 2 tablespoons tomato paste
- 1 tablespoon chili powder
- 1 teaspoon ground cumin
- 1 teaspoon dried oregano
- 1/2 teaspoon smoked paprika
- Salt and pepper to taste
- Optional toppings: Shredded cheese, sour cream, chopped fresh cilantro, diced avocado, sliced green onions, or tortilla chips

Instructions:

1. Heat olive oil in a large pot or Dutch oven over medium heat.
2. Add the chopped onion and cook for 2-3 minutes until softened.
3. Stir in the minced garlic and cook for another 1-2 minutes until fragrant.
4. Add the chopped bell pepper to the pot and cook for 2-3 minutes until slightly softened.
5. Stir in the drained and rinsed black beans, kidney beans, and pinto beans.
6. Add the diced tomatoes (with their juices), vegetable broth or water, tomato paste, chili powder, ground cumin, dried oregano, smoked paprika, salt, and pepper to the pot. Stir well to combine.
7. Bring the chili to a simmer, then reduce the heat to low. Cover and let it simmer for 20-25 minutes, stirring occasionally, to allow the flavors to meld together and the chili to thicken.
8. Once done, taste the chili and adjust the seasoning with more salt and pepper if needed.

9. Serve the three bean chili hot, topped with your favorite toppings such as shredded cheese, sour cream, chopped fresh cilantro, diced avocado, sliced green onions, or tortilla chips.
10. Enjoy your delicious and comforting three bean chili!

Feel free to customize this recipe by adding other ingredients such as corn, diced tomatoes with green chilies, or additional spices to suit your taste preferences. You can also make this chili ahead of time and store it in the refrigerator for a few days, or freeze it for longer storage. It's a versatile and satisfying dish that's perfect for meal prep or feeding a crowd.

Mashed Potatoes with Gravy

Ingredients:

- 2 pounds (about 4 large) russet potatoes, peeled and cut into chunks
- 4 tablespoons unsalted butter
- 1/2 cup milk or heavy cream
- Salt and pepper to taste
- Chopped fresh parsley for garnish (optional)

Instructions:

1. Place the peeled and chopped potatoes in a large pot and cover them with cold water.
2. Bring the water to a boil over high heat, then reduce the heat to medium-low and simmer for 15-20 minutes, or until the potatoes are fork-tender.
3. Drain the cooked potatoes and return them to the pot.
4. Add the butter to the pot with the potatoes, and mash them using a potato masher until smooth and creamy.
5. Gradually add the milk or heavy cream to the mashed potatoes, stirring until the desired consistency is reached. You may need more or less milk depending on your preference.
6. Season the mashed potatoes with salt and pepper to taste, and stir well to combine.
7. Transfer the mashed potatoes to a serving dish, garnish with chopped fresh parsley if desired, and keep warm until ready to serve.

Gravy:

Ingredients:

- 2 tablespoons unsalted butter
- 2 tablespoons all-purpose flour
- 1 cup beef or chicken broth
- Salt and pepper to taste

Instructions:

1. In a small saucepan, melt the butter over medium heat.
2. Add the flour to the melted butter, stirring constantly to form a smooth paste (roux).
3. Cook the roux for 1-2 minutes, stirring constantly, until it turns golden brown.

4. Gradually add the beef or chicken broth to the saucepan, whisking constantly to prevent lumps from forming.
5. Bring the gravy to a simmer, then reduce the heat to low and cook for 2-3 minutes, or until the gravy thickens to your desired consistency.
6. Season the gravy with salt and pepper to taste, and stir well to combine.
7. Once done, remove the gravy from heat and keep warm until ready to serve.

Serving:

- Serve the mashed potatoes hot, topped with the warm gravy.

Enjoy your delicious mashed potatoes with gravy as a comforting and satisfying side dish!

Tofu Scramble with Spinach

Ingredients:

- 1 block (14-16 ounces) firm tofu, drained and pressed
- 2 tablespoons olive oil
- 1 small onion, diced
- 2 cloves garlic, minced
- 1 teaspoon ground turmeric
- 1 teaspoon ground cumin
- 1/2 teaspoon ground paprika
- Salt and pepper to taste
- 2 cups fresh spinach leaves, chopped
- Optional add-ins: diced bell peppers, sliced mushrooms, cherry tomatoes, or chopped green onions
- Optional toppings: chopped fresh cilantro, sliced avocado, or hot sauce

Instructions:

1. Prepare the tofu: Drain the tofu and place it between paper towels or clean kitchen towels. Place a heavy object on top (such as a cast-iron skillet or a few heavy books) to press out excess moisture for about 15-20 minutes. Once pressed, crumble the tofu into small pieces with your hands or a fork.
2. Heat olive oil in a large skillet or frying pan over medium heat.
3. Add the diced onion to the skillet and cook for 2-3 minutes until softened.
4. Stir in the minced garlic and cook for another minute until fragrant.
5. Add the crumbled tofu to the skillet, and sprinkle ground turmeric, ground cumin, ground paprika, salt, and pepper over the tofu. Stir well to coat the tofu evenly with the spices.
6. Cook the tofu for 5-6 minutes, stirring occasionally, until heated through and lightly browned.
7. Stir in the chopped fresh spinach leaves and any optional add-ins (such as diced bell peppers, sliced mushrooms, cherry tomatoes, or chopped green onions). Cook for an additional 2-3 minutes, or until the spinach is wilted and any additional vegetables are tender.
8. Taste and adjust the seasoning with more salt and pepper if needed.
9. Once done, remove the skillet from heat and serve the tofu scramble hot.
10. Garnish with optional toppings such as chopped fresh cilantro, sliced avocado, or hot sauce, if desired.
11. Enjoy your delicious and nutritious tofu scramble with spinach!

This tofu scramble is versatile, and you can customize it with your favorite vegetables, herbs, and spices. Serve it with toast, tortillas, or alongside roasted potatoes for a satisfying meal.

Peanut Noodles

Ingredients:

- 8 ounces (about 225 grams) spaghetti or noodles of your choice
- 1/4 cup creamy peanut butter
- 3 tablespoons soy sauce
- 2 tablespoons rice vinegar
- 1 tablespoon sesame oil
- 1 tablespoon honey or maple syrup
- 1 clove garlic, minced
- 1 teaspoon grated ginger
- 1/4 teaspoon red pepper flakes (adjust to taste)
- 2 green onions, thinly sliced
- Optional toppings: Chopped peanuts, sesame seeds, sliced green onions, chopped cilantro, or lime wedges

Instructions:

1. Cook the spaghetti or noodles according to the package instructions until al dente. Drain and rinse under cold water to stop the cooking process. Set aside.
2. In a medium mixing bowl, whisk together the creamy peanut butter, soy sauce, rice vinegar, sesame oil, honey or maple syrup, minced garlic, grated ginger, and red pepper flakes until smooth and well combined. If the sauce is too thick, you can add a splash of warm water to thin it out to your desired consistency.
3. Add the cooked and drained noodles to the bowl with the peanut sauce. Toss well to coat the noodles evenly with the sauce.
4. Garnish the peanut noodles with sliced green onions and any optional toppings you like, such as chopped peanuts, sesame seeds, chopped cilantro, or lime wedges.
5. Serve the peanut noodles immediately, or refrigerate them for at least 30 minutes to allow the flavors to meld together and serve them chilled.
6. Enjoy your delicious and flavorful peanut noodles as a satisfying meal or side dish!

Feel free to customize this recipe by adding other ingredients such as thinly sliced bell peppers, shredded carrots, chopped cucumber, or cooked chicken or tofu for added protein. Peanut noodles are versatile and can be enjoyed hot, cold, or at room temperature, making them a great option for meal prep or picnics.

Rice and Beans Burritos

Ingredients:

- 1 cup cooked rice (white or brown)
- 1 can (15 ounces) black beans, drained and rinsed
- 1 cup salsa (store-bought or homemade)
- 1 teaspoon ground cumin
- 1 teaspoon chili powder
- Salt and pepper to taste
- 4 large flour tortillas
- Optional fillings: Shredded cheese, diced tomatoes, diced avocado, chopped cilantro, sliced green onions, sour cream, or hot sauce

Instructions:

1. In a medium saucepan, combine the cooked rice, black beans, salsa, ground cumin, and chili powder. Cook over medium heat for 5-7 minutes, stirring occasionally, until heated through and well combined. Season with salt and pepper to taste.
2. Warm the flour tortillas in the microwave or in a dry skillet for a few seconds to make them pliable.
3. Divide the rice and beans mixture evenly among the flour tortillas, placing it in the center of each tortilla.
4. Add any optional fillings you like, such as shredded cheese, diced tomatoes, diced avocado, chopped cilantro, sliced green onions, sour cream, or hot sauce.
5. Fold the sides of each tortilla over the filling, then fold the bottom edge up and over the filling, and roll tightly to form a burrito.
6. Repeat with the remaining tortillas and filling to make additional burritos.
7. Serve the rice and beans burritos immediately, or wrap them tightly in aluminum foil and keep warm in a low oven until ready to serve.
8. Enjoy your delicious and flavorful rice and beans burritos!

These rice and beans burritos are versatile, and you can customize them with your favorite fillings and toppings. They're perfect for a quick and satisfying meal that's packed with protein and fiber. Serve them with extra salsa, guacamole, or a side salad for a complete meal.

Baked Falafel Wraps

Ingredients:

For the Baked Falafel:

- 1 can (15 ounces) chickpeas, drained and rinsed
- 1/4 cup chopped fresh parsley
- 1/4 cup chopped fresh cilantro
- 2 cloves garlic, minced
- 1 small onion, chopped
- 1 teaspoon ground cumin
- 1 teaspoon ground coriander
- 1/2 teaspoon baking powder
- 2 tablespoons all-purpose flour
- Salt and pepper to taste
- Olive oil for brushing

For Assembling the Wraps:

- 4 large whole wheat or spinach wraps
- Hummus (store-bought or homemade)
- Tzatziki sauce (store-bought or homemade)
- Sliced cucumbers
- Sliced tomatoes
- Sliced red onion
- Shredded lettuce or spinach leaves
- Optional toppings: Chopped fresh parsley, chopped fresh cilantro, sliced olives, crumbled feta cheese, or hot sauce

Instructions:

For the Baked Falafel:

1. Preheat your oven to 375°F (190°C). Line a baking sheet with parchment paper or lightly grease it with olive oil.
2. In a food processor, combine the chickpeas, chopped fresh parsley, chopped fresh cilantro, minced garlic, chopped onion, ground cumin, ground coriander, baking powder, all-purpose flour, salt, and pepper. Pulse until the mixture is well combined but still slightly chunky.
3. Shape the falafel mixture into small patties or balls using your hands.

4. Place the shaped falafel patties or balls on the prepared baking sheet, spacing them apart.
5. Brush the tops of the falafel with olive oil.
6. Bake in the preheated oven for 20-25 minutes, or until the falafel is golden brown and crispy on the outside.
7. Once done, remove the falafel from the oven and let them cool slightly before assembling the wraps.

For Assembling the Wraps:

1. Spread a generous layer of hummus on each wrap, leaving a border around the edges.
2. Top the hummus with a few slices of cucumber, tomato, and red onion.
3. Add a few falafel patties or balls to each wrap.
4. Drizzle with tzatziki sauce.
5. Add a handful of shredded lettuce or spinach leaves on top.
6. Sprinkle with optional toppings such as chopped fresh parsley, chopped fresh cilantro, sliced olives, crumbled feta cheese, or hot sauce, if desired.
7. Fold the sides of each wrap over the filling, then roll tightly to form a wrap.
8. Repeat with the remaining wraps and filling to make additional wraps.
9. Serve the baked falafel wraps immediately, or wrap them tightly in aluminum foil and refrigerate until ready to serve.
10. Enjoy your delicious and satisfying baked falafel wraps!

These baked falafel wraps are perfect for a quick and healthy lunch or dinner. They're customizable, so feel free to add your favorite toppings and sauces to suit your taste preferences.

www.ingramcontent.com/pod-product-compliance
Lightning Source LLC
LaVergne TN
LVHW081614060526
838201LV00054B/2246